conversations with ghosts

the ghost

CONVERSATIONS WITH GHOSTS
revised and expanded edition
copyright © 2019-2023 by ryan donnelly
all rights reserved
no part of this book may be used or reproduced in any manner whatsoever without written permission except in the case of brief quotations embodied in critical articles and reviews
for more information, email author

---

email: thetroubledmonk@gmail.com
instagram: @thetroubledmonk

conversations with ghosts

ryan donnelly

dedication

i must dedicate this book to three separate sources

firstly
to the ones who have had to offer me their hope
in times when love left me running on empty

secondly
to all of you
beautiful *loves* of my life
i hope that each one of you is taking care of that piece
of my heart that i left you all with
whether you wanted to keep it or not
and even though we never made it
at least we tried
right?

and finally
to that tiny stubborn ember that resides inside of me
the one that never fully burns out
the one that demands that i still believe in love
and better days ahead
that little ember that i call '*hope*'

'*thank you for sticking around just a little longer*'

i sat across from you today

    after so many years of learning the curves of your body

i stared into those incredibly familiar eyes of yours

    and i have never felt so alone

forward
by ryan donnelly

---

*T*he book you are now holding in your hands is what I consider to be proof of how much art can be used as therapy in one's life, and it is a true testament to how often the words that I write are words that I have difficulty speaking out loud.

I wrote this book during a time when my life was experiencing a great transformation. I had once again found myself single after, yet another, failed attempt at a relationship that would last, but this time around something was different, not only was I older and a bit wiser, but this time I felt as if the lessons of my past were showing up as gifts to help me weather this storm in a better way than all those heartbroken times before.

This is not to say that I wasn't underneath the weight of both sadness and anger, because with loss, unexpected change, and with the death of love, these two always rush in to provide some of the company that you will be forced to keep as you heal through your pain.

I felt as if this time I could talk to those ghosts of my past, this time I wouldn't just hold my pain inside and wear my sadness as a smile, I wouldn't just hold onto that feeling of melancholy and rage, this time I would also carry hope, reason, and understanding with me as well.

Historically speaking, I have never been the greatest at letting go of love without first pointing the finger directly at the one that I loved.

They needed to know that their betrayals changed me and that their ability to turn off their emotions as coldly as one would turn off a light switch had confused, infuriated, and corrupted me to my core. Each one of those that I gave my heart to would take a piece that I would never get back, and what I felt I was given in return was something much darker and heavier to carry with me for the years that would follow.

In those times I wasn't ready to take responsibility for my part in the ending of our unions, but as I stated above, this time I saw the gifts that my past was forcing me to see, I was becoming aware of the truth of my chosen place among the heartbroken, and I knew that I had judged them all far too harshly because this time I could see the part that I played in the destruction of my relationships as well.

I could see that the trade we had made was not as one-sided as I had led myself to believe and that I left them changed as well, and I could not, and I would not continue to lie to myself and continue to act as if I had left them with less than their own sense of loss and transformation.

This book arrived in my heart when I was ready to acknowledge and accept the truth of love and change. It manifested itself into reality when I became open to the idea that I may have been somewhat instrumental in the pain that I had to endure.
This diary of sorts only spoke to me when I was ready to acknowledge the gifts that all transformation brings with it, no matter the gravity of one's own wounded heart.

When I sat down in that coffee shop to start writing this book one thing was clear to me, it was time to have those conversations with my ghosts, not because I was still sinking beneath the emotional weight of my past, but because I was now ready to let go of day-old pain and impossible stories to make way for something much greater: *gratitude* and *hope*.

preface

i am writing this with a wounded heart
yet again

it seems that i am still addicted to fucking things up
but trust me when i say that it is not for a lack of trying
to get love right for once

if you are reading this
then chances are
you have had love and you have lost it
perhaps
even multiple times

if so
then these poems are for you
because they are for the broken but still hopeful

they are for the lost and the defeated
they are for anyone who finds themselves still having
conversations with ghosts

contents

i
the deal that i made   1
if i'm being honest   2
goodbye for you but not for me   3
honeybee   4
new love   5
the gambler   6
it was you and i until it wasn't   7
love is   8
where are you hiding it?   9
disarm   10
is it too much to ask for?   11
the hard truth   12
the change   13
i know   14
opposites attract   15
marionette   16
where did we go?   17
tall café latte, please   18
it is what it is   19
she doesn't see me   20
what i started with   21
unclear   22
still
eyes wide fucked   23
we can hurt each other now   24
the words that i said   25
my love loves another   26
where is your light now?   27
history repeats itself   28
i told you this was hard on me   29
only a friend   30
the script   31
the grip   32

contents

like an ant hitting a wall   33
you have it wrong   34
maybe   35
the mistakes that i make   36
laid to rest   37
screaming love   38
i wish that i could   39
the mess that you made   40
storms are coming   41
why say it at all now?   42
only you   43
homesick   44
my love is a wounded animal   45
fucked   46
the rope   47-48
you are the one   49
hope is a dangerous thing   50
rain on my cheek   51-52
i want you to smile   53
the gravity of it all   54
falling on a fall day   55-56
penance   57
can you remind me?   58
eventually   59
underneath it all   60
hope on empty   61
we want the same thing   62
here we go again   63
do i have to say goodbye?   64
it's not you it's how you feel   65
i see you everywhere now   66
i am still here   67
i think i might know how you felt   68
it's what i do   69

contents

outrun you   70-71
have
heaven and hell   72
the honeymoon phase   73
regrets   74
is it that time yet?   75-76
the sacrifice   77
warning   78
please   79
let me hold that for you   80
calypso   81
an attempt was made   82
these walls do not house a home   83
let it burn   84
hope protects you   85
the hunting darkness   86
the weight   87
my heart has turned   88
pandora   89
eventually   90
remember what mother said   91
feet off the floor   92
fool me once   93
undone   94
sour   95
this is how it goes   96
we could try   97
i can't stay here   98
you will be missed   99
just one more conversation   100
lying in wait   101
gemma   102
time and space   103
love is like   104

contents

it happens over time   105
wish you were here   106
out there   107
never forget   108
write this down   109
keep this in mind   110
it's there   111
water in my lungs   112
not ready to care   113
don't you see?   114
your side   115
our contract   116
i know it's not good   117
the fear   118
where are you?   119
ghost therapy   120-121
hope

conversations with ghosts

i

conversations with ghosts

the deal that i made

this blank page is asking for far too many of my secrets

if i'm being honest

i am already exhausted by this sadness
and the worst part is
this is only the beginning

goodbye for you but not for me

you left today
i wanted to say *goodbye*
and truly mean it

but i know this flawed heart of mine
and even though you left today
i know that i am still going to be right here
still having these conversations with your ghost

honeybee

i always thought that honeybees were the nice ones
who was it that told me that they don't sting?

i think it was you

you also showed me
that when they sting
they kill

new love

you weren't ready
i knew that
but i wanted more

you were wounded and scared
and i was afraid that you might disappear if i opened my heart to you

we both know that you almost did

you weren't ready
and if i am being honest here
i am not quite sure that i was either

but everyone knows that new love requires a bit of hope and faith

now
you are gone
and i was right about you

the gambler

you are no gambler you say
but you choose to love
right?

ignoring the fatal chances that you take
whenever you choose to open your heart to another
does nothing to hide what i see

i say that you are the biggest gambler of them all
for the stakes that you play for are for the very things
that you can never have back again

it was you and i until it wasn't

i sat across from you today
after so many years of shared love and trust
i stared into your familiar eyes
but you stared right through mine

we always came back to pick the other one up from imminent defeat
we always washed the blood off each other's worn-out spirits
we always tried to work it out

you said that you needed nothing more
i said that i loved that about you
and i always knew that you were hiding the truth

two can never become one
they can only ever walk beside one another
we can only ever share in our loneliness alone
there must always be a division line
and that is what makes us one

i sat across from you today
after so many years of learning the curves of your body
i stared into those incredibly familiar eyes of yours
and i have never felt so alone

love is

true love always brings the potential of self-destruction to bed with it

where are you hiding it?

can a heart as scarred as mine ever stop looking for the knife that i know you must be hiding from me?

disarm

remember when we both knew that we would
overcome everything that life would throw at us?
i miss the innocence found in the days that were always
numbered for you and i

looking back now...
i think we were always looking back

locked in a silent knife fight
you always knew how to disarm me
and now there is no overcoming what life is throwing
my way
because it is using you against me this time around
and we both know that i never could disarm you

is it too much to ask for?

---

they say that life is only a series of *'hellos'* and *'goodbyes'*

do you think we might ever get the chance to say *'hello'* one more time?

i always did ask for too much
didn't i?

the hard truth

i see time etched upon my face
far too few laugh lines can be seen now
just fear
and loss
and cracks deep enough for the rest of my hope to get lost in

i can see time chiseling away at the best of me
and leaving behind
only the worst of you

the change

you were my first
and your deception paved the way for the rest

you were the first
and i knew that no one would ever escape the sight of
that scar that you left on my heart

you were the first
and you showed me what i am worth
i just wish you had thought more of me

the next ones came in
and they found that untrusting scar of mine
and when they left
they added their personalized cuts right beside yours

and now
i am starting to look a lot more like the ones who
placed those scars on your own heart so long ago

i know

i know
that my heart is not the first to be left behind by the changing of another's
i know
that my love was not the first to suffer the poison of deceit
i know
that i am not the only one who has been forced to watch as their lover's gaze glazed over with unspoken tears for the end
i know
that i will find another who will entice me to take one more chance on something i am not meant to keep
i know
that i am not alone in all this
and yet
has anyone ever felt this alone?

opposites attract

you were oil
i was water
and no amount of fucking would have ever mixed us
together forever

marionette

i always could see the strings attached to everything in
this world full of puppets
falling in love with one another
trying so very hard to fall in love with the right one
building their futures in fear
trying to overcome those fears
trying to forget those fears
and eventually
succumbing to all those fears

becoming ghosts locked in the past
hopelessly still attached by a loving filament from one
heart to another
and this one string connected from your heart to mine
can never be severed
no matter how hard i fucking try

where did we go?

remember when we thought that we could build a future on quicksand?

those were the good days

tall café latte, please

---

this room is full of people trying not to look so lonely

it is what it is

i was hoping that i had done enough good to protect
myself from moments like this
as if karma were a real thing
as if the universe wasn't so impersonal
as if i deserved to smile
even one day more

i was hopeful that you had left your old ways behind
you
as if you could burn that little black book with all their
horrible names written inside
as if you could go even one day alone with your own
thoughts
as if i could ever have been enough for you

i was hoping that hope would be enough
as if hope had the strength to override reality
as if hope could burn little black books
as if the words '*i love you*' might mean something more
than just those three overused and empty words

she doesn't see me

she undresses in front of me
and i can tell that she is no longer undressing for me
she is looking right through me now
and i can feel that she doesn't even see me anymore
it is clear to me that i am only taking up space
where another should be

she lays on our bed
and i can tell that she no longer desires to lay beside me
she no longer lays close enough to feel the heat from
my body
and i can tell that she doesn't want to hear my heartbeat
any longer next to hers
i know that i am only taking up the space
where she now desires him to be

she says
'you know that i love you'
and i can tell that she is being impulsive again

she might not see me
but she has not heard from him lately
and now all she can see is fear
and it is fear that has always cured my invisibility

what i started with

it started with a *hope* and a *prayer*
and now that she is gone
i am giving both of them right back

unclear

you and i tried to reach a dream
we tried so hard to reach the sun itself
but whose dream was it anyway?
i can't remember wanting anything anymore

all i can recall is the venom that dripped from your last
'i love you'

along with the smell of our
once hopeful
burnt wings

conversations with ghosts

still

eyes wide fucked

i blocked you on social media the moment that you ran away
i didn't want to know what you were up to
or who was in your bed these days

i had no desire to watch you build another life without me

in this world of perpetual ruin and heartache
i wanted to give myself the best chance at being happy
but then i made the mistake of closing my eyes
and there you were

we can hurt each other now

before you disappear
before i run away
before our emotions get caught in an undertow and
pulled out into the empty ocean
just know that i never meant to show you that i cared
that much
when i already knew that you had given up on us

i wanted to save you from my disappointment
i wanted to continue to hide behind my fake smile
for just a little while longer anyway

i wanted to protect your heart for just one moment
more
but you kept forgetting who i was to you
and your words are out of control now
and your words are heat seeking-knives
aimed straight at my already scarred heart

and now
all i want to do is show you how much i care
because i know how much it kills you

the words that i said

she looked at me for approval of her new love
after all
if you love someone
their happiness is the most important thing of all

she waited for my blessing of her tryst
after all
she knew that i loved her enough to want to see her
happy

she was patient enough for me to formulate some
words
and i could tell that she wasn't ready to know the truth
that maybe i didn't love her that much anymore

my love loves another

she is excited about her new love interest
she waits for him to contact her
she buys new clothes and works out hard for him
she sees the man that she wants to build a future with
in him
she offers up infinite reasons for why he doesn't
contact her as much as she wants him to
she is head over heels for a man she thinks she knows
she wants to make all the right moves for him
she wishes he would come to take her far away from
the life she built here with me

she tells me all these things
and why wouldn't she?
i am the man that she has always confided in
i am her best friend

and I am supposed to be there for her
right?

where is your light now?

a heart like mine can love the misfits
the broken
the lost
the hopeless
the wounded
the hollow
the faithless
the cynical
and the abandoned

a heart like mine will always search for the light in the darkness
and right now
i am so very lost just trying to love you

history repeats itself

here i am
again
staring my history
right in the ugly face

wishing that i could have developed a better sense of
what impossible means

but i am far too stubborn
and i have this unyielding sense of hope
and i am far too nice to willingly break her heart

so i just wait until she eventually breaks mine

i told you this was hard on me

is it so hard to believe that losing you might be the end of that side of me that you loved so much?

only a friend

i saw the way that he looked at you
i caught that sidelong glance that he shot your way
when he thought that i wasn't looking
but i never stop looking for a thief in a room
or a wolf at the door
and deception always smells the same anyway

you tell me that *'he is only a friend'*
but i know you better than that
and you know that i do
a lie from a lover always finds its way into the spotlight

i know that it's just a slip of the tongue
because after seeing the bitemarks that he left on your neck
i know that those words you spoke about him
were really meant for me

the script

you apologized for hurting me
but i know that you didn't mean to
i just don't know how to tell you that it's alright

it's not your fault that the boy always loses the girl
as it's not your fault that i continue taking chances with
my heart

the grip

i didn't quite understand the true power of fear until
you took off the ring that i gave you for the potential
future with another
and still
you ask me if we might
one day
find our way back to each other?

and i still find myself secretly wanting to say
'yes'

like an ant hitting a wall

i know that one day your ghost won't haunt me
so completely

just as i know
that one day
i won't let the smell of your perfume on a stranger
passing me by
lead me to another drink

you have it wrong

---

i stayed silent as you talked about him
they said that i was patient

i held back my tears as you disconnected your emotions from us
you said that it was clear that i would be just fine

i still held you close as you struggled with the change
you said that i was so strong

from your lips
defeat sounds so very impressive

maybe

you said that you would never leave
and i said that i believed you
we never could tell each other the whole truth
could we?

you said that the ring i gave you felt like home
but i could tell that it was getting heavier for you as our days marched on
we will look back and say that we tried
another half-truth to be sure

you said that it wasn't about all those things
but i can see that *he* is all those *things*
you never could lie worth shit to me

i could see this day coming from a mile away
and i know that you could too
our love would never have found a way to carry the weight of that temperamental ring

and now
we try our luck at one final lie…
maybe we can find a way to still be friends?

the mistakes that i make

if i could ask you one thing
my love
i would ask that you never forget how much i love you

as time passes
and it always does
as it steals the fearful and exciting pulse of new love
from us every new day
as it always will
just remember how my heart beats for you now

as our days must always turn into nights
and our long kisses shorten
just a little bit more each day
don't you dare forget this promise to me

now
i am just a ghost looking back through a rearview
mirror
to see if you are still there to talk to

i want to ask you if you kept your promise to me
but you are no longer there anymore
you are no longer anywhere at all
and i now see the fatal mistake that i made

i should have made you promise not to forget how
much you loved me

laid to rest

there was a time
long ago
when you chased me down so fiercely

a time when you loved me so much that you patiently
waited as i chased all the others

i didn't know what i could have had
i didn't see what could have been
and still
you waited for the day when i might see you
a day when i might finally see us

you got your wish
and we loved the way that you always desired
but dreams so often fade in time
and ours became a series of broken mirrors
venomous words
and regrets

you should know that our love was the first funeral that
my heart ever attended

screaming love

Seeing you there across the counter with your pixie cut
and that devious makeup on
i tried to play it cool
you did too

i left you a hopeful letter and left
you chased me out the door to an empty street
i figured you might have done that
which is why i waited so long to return

when i came back to see you again
it culminated in an explosion of lust
fucking
and fighting

our love was a great and terrible thing
for both of us

like a sexy knife fight with your best friend
with the only rule being to aim straight for the other's heart

i wish that i could

i wanted to smash your fucking heart into a million pieces for the way that you treated me as you left

but then i remembered that he would be there to help pick all those pieces back up with you once i was gone

the mess that you made

you used to drive me mad with your ability to create a mess
how many fights did we have over just the makeup on the counter?
the paint all over the garage?
and the random clothes tossed carelessly on the floor?
far too many

you know
my love
now that you are gone
and i am left cleaning up the mess that you made
i just wish you would show up once more
and throw even more clothes on the floor

what i am trying to tell you is that i am going to miss you

storms are coming

two ships we were
adrift and lost at sea
we crashed into one another
over and over and over again

nothing in the world could sink us
nothing could change our course
we had such fear of losing one another that it honestly
felt like this shared fear might bind us together forever
or at least i had hoped as much

then
over time
i stopped watching what your hands were doing while
we held each other close
distracted by the touching of our lips

now i see
that you were untying the knot in our rope as we kissed
and now here we are
once again
two ships adrift and lost at sea
just praying to crash into someone else one day

why say it at all now?

you said '*i love you*'
even after you walked away from us and all that we were
and all that we could have been

and now i am left to wonder just what love might *actually*
mean to you?

only you

i am the one
and so are you…
for now

homesick

underneath the deception
the lies
the secrets
the pain
the sadness
the emptiness
the loss
the betrayal
the-every-terrible-fucking-thing that you put my heart through
i still chased your love with all that i had left
i still left the light on for you
and all in the hope that you might one day come back home

all because i still believed in love

but i don't anymore
and the light is no longer on for you

my love is a wounded animal

when i found you
you were broken and scared

i gave you a safe place to heal your wounds
i fed you a healthy diet of love and respect

i nurtured you away from the lonely corner that you hid in
i watched as you stepped out into the sun once again
so full of love

when i found you
you were broken and scared
and now you are gone
because love is a trap for you
and i think that i was starting to look a lot like the one
who wounded you once before

fucked

---

our compromise has been compromised

the rope

where did you go *hope*?
did i forget to bring you along with me this time?
i know
sometimes i can be so bloody distracted

she seems to be doing just fine without me now
did you decide that her company was better than mine?
sometimes *hope* you can be such a fucking asshole

was there something more i could have done to keep
you with me just a little bit longer?
or was her offer to you as tempting as his was to her?
will you ever be coming back?
are you even listening to me anymore?

she suffered the darkest of days
her mind forever a dance between the future and the
end
and when she asked where the rope was
i told her that i hid it far away

hope
my old friend
it has become clear to me that you have a hard time
being with both of us at the same time

i endured all our fears because i had you with me
i weathered the many storms that came our way
challenged them even
and all because you once listened to me

now
i am trying to find just where you went
before i remember where i hid that fucking rope

you are the one

my love is forever
but the new ones never want you to feel that way

every beautiful soul that i have ever loved has kept a
piece of my heart

as will the next one

and i will have to hide that fact
as i always do
because new love never wants to hear that you ever felt
that way

hope is a dangerous thing

i hope that i won't always feel this way
but now that you are gone
and i am left sinking in this loneliness
all i can do is try to remind myself that love lost means
love still yet to be found

i hope that i won't always be this way
but now that history has repeated itself
and i am left staring into the mirror
all i can do is ask myself *'what am i learning about myself
from all of this heartache?'*

i hope that i won't always hope that you might come
back home to me
but i know myself
and i have a hard time seeing beyond your best qualities
and all i can do now is burn our house down in the
hope that i can protect myself from the potential of you
and i

rain on my cheek

i have been trying as hard as i can not to break down and cry
i keep running away from reality by hiding in random coffee shops
just staring out the window to nothing at all

i try to make eye contact with beautiful strangers
but i am far too broken now
and far too shy
and sadly
still not over you
and i need to be alone
even if i don't want to be

we never made this our coffee shop
but the roads to get here we have traveled a thousand times before
and they are filled with our ghosts of those better days
and if i am being honest about it
i sometimes dream about forcing myself violently off the road
but i still have this damn hope inside me that you always loved about me so much

now i am staring out the window of this coffee shop once again
focusing on nothing really
just the blue sky and sunny days that you loved so very much

it's a strange thing

but i think that it might have started raining inside just now

i want you to smile

you messaged me today and asked me how i was doing

you won't ever know just how much i wanted to tell you the truth

but i didn't want to ruin your day

the gravity of it all

you were never my sun
my moon
or my stars

my love
you were always so much more than that

falling on a fall day

it was the most beautiful day
and even though i knew that we were heading for the end
i still hoped
with all that i had left
that we could avoid falling apart
like everyone else does

you asked me if i would ever marry you
i said *'of course i will'*
and in case you were wondering
i did notice how your eyes flickered with sadness at my response
in truth
i never forgot that moment
and i know that you didn't either

the dead leaves fell all around us
just as defeated as we were
but the sun defied the clouds
much like my heart defied the truth
and we held each other close
the way that friends do at a funeral

eventually
you found your way out of our agreement
and all it cost was how i would forever look at you
this time it was you that would now have to witness the flicker of sadness in my eyes
and you won't forget it
i promise you

we are so far away from that beautiful sunny fall day
and yet
i am right back there now
because today i asked her if she still wanted to get married

penance

i'm spilling my heart out all over this page for the chance to say something right for a change

can you remind me?

do you remember when i smiled and laughed
and filled your heart with so much joy
and love that is spilled all over the place?

those days are long gone by now
back when we knew that all we would ever need
was each other

do you remember those days at all?

because i am starting to forget what a laugh even
sounds like

eventually

i'm afraid of holding onto beautiful things for too long because i know that eventually i always break them

underneath it all

my love
i never lied to you
i never kept secrets from you
but lately, i have been secretly practicing how to say
goodbye to you

hope on empty

i get through everything because i have always had hope
nothing more
nothing less
just hope

and hope is enough
it has to be

we want the same thing

they want to see you smile
just like you once did
before you lost the one that you believed might have
always been

they want you to feel happiness
just like you once did
before you could no longer even stand to touch
fingertips

they want you to feel hope
the way that you once did
back when two lovers wishfully said
'i love you'
and truly meant it

and i understand
because i want that to

here we go again

the one who came before you
broke me
the one before her
broke me too
the one before that
broke me as well

and you
you are playing your part perfectly

do i have to say goodbye?

i want to keep writing these words down for you
you know that i always had far too much to say

i could sit here in front of this hungry notepad forever
because right now this feels like the only way that i get
to talk to you honestly anymore

it's not you it's how you feel

i hate that you don't love me enough to stay

i see you everywhere now

i thought that i saw you on the street today
yesterday i thought that i saw you leaving this coffee
shop in a hurry
it's unnerving to feel you everywhere that i go
never seeing you completely
just flashes of your image disappearing as soon as i take
notice of you

i want to chase you down
i want to tell you to stop haunting me
i want to tell you that i still love you
i want to show you how much better i have become
since you went away
but i am worse
so much worse
and you are right to keep disappearing on me

i am still here

i have never been any good at saying *goodbye*

which is why i am still trying to find ways to see you once again

i was hoping that you could teach me a little about how to give up on love

i think i might know how you felt

the faint smell of freshly brewed coffee in the morning
always woke you up
to be honest
that's why i would always make it for you
if i didn't
you would never have left our bed

now
no one is here to make coffee for me
and i don't see myself leaving this bed any time soon

my love
just how long have you been this sad?

it's what i do

i have always worn my sadness like a smile

outrun you

i used to run as fast as i could away from all the heartache
but you always had a nasty habit of tracking me down
no matter what dark corner i tried to hide away in

all i ever wanted to do was escape the pain of looking at your beautiful face
of hearing your familiar voice
and of smelling your intoxicating perfume

all i ever wanted to do
was just keep running
as fast and as far as i could
but you always seemed to find a way back to me

we both know that i would try to run just slow enough
that you might still find me
i didn't want to see you
but i could never imagine never seeing you again

many years later
i sat with you
but it wasn't the *you* that i once ran from
i scanned your face in secret as you said something to me
but i wasn't really listening
i was just trying to see the woman that i once knew and loved so much within that time-touched face
hints of you could be seen
but no flashes of love could be felt anymore

not for this stranger who forgot to continue to love the
boy who never stopped running
i didn't stay long with you
i said that i had some important business to attend to
but we both knew that i was still on the run

this time i wasn't going to take a chance of letting the
past ever catch up to me again
this time i wasn't going to slow my pace for anyone at
all

the past can have you now

conversations with ghosts

have

heaven and hell

when one heart becomes two
it is heaven

when two hearts become three
it is hell

the honeymoon phase

i won't always be the best-looking guy in the room to you
i won't always tell you jokes that make you laugh out loud
i won't always make your heart skip a beat when you see me
i won't always inspire you to dream about the future
i won't always be strong enough for you to lean on
i won't always be everything that you think you need

there will come a time
when i will come to be the person that you know better than yourself
and when you see just how human i can be

there will come a time
when i will need you to be there for me
in the same way that i have always been there for you

what will you do when that time comes?
will you still see me?
or will you see someone else instead?

i fear that i might know the answer

regrets

wait
before you go i want to tell you that i think you are making a terrible mistake

i should have said this to you as you walked away

and you should have looked back one last time

is it that time yet?

my phone vibrates on the table
it's late in the day
which is how i know that it's you
i get it
i miss you too

how long has it been since we went an entire day
without talking to each other?
it feels like forever now
i fear your potential text as much as i hopefully wait for it
this new loneliness feels too much like purgatory for me

you ask me heartfelt questions
like '*how am i doing?*' or '*are things getting better for me?*'
i know that you still truly care
which is why it hurts me so much when i can't stop
myself from throwing some venom your way

i only ever wanted to be enough for you
and now that you are gone
no words need to be said
but to the broken reflection in the mirror
i say it straight
'*i fucked up again*'
i know that one day the phone will stop reminding me
that you care
because one day he will find you
or you will find him
and you will no longer need the comfort of knowing
that i am still here

thinking about us
i know how this goes
eventually
after enough time passes
you will take your place
and join with all the other ghosts that still haunt me

the sacrifice

i know that you are out there
somewhere
waking up with a desire to laugh more

you are working out
and then dressing up
making the most of your new life

you are eating oatmeal for breakfast
and sushi for lunch
in the evening you are having a few social drinks with
your new friends

it will be a day to remember
and tomorrow is going to be even better
and all you had to do was give up the life that we were
building together

you sound confident about your choice through a
message
then i hear it in your voice
and it's right then that i can tell that you see us again

but the sacrifice has already been made
and cupid has no more arrows left for us

warning

i love how you met such a perfect man for you
because i remember a time when i was him
and we both know how that worked out

some advice for you *my love*

this time don't make the mistake of forgetting that your
love will always
eventually
need saving from the ordinary march of time

please

wake me up when my heart finally forgets about you

let me hold that for you

both of us need to carry a red flag for a while
signaling to other potential lovers that we are not yet
ready to be loved

but don't you worry
i will hold yours for you while you go fuck someone
else

calypso

not every love worth remembering has years attached
to it

sometimes
you are lucky enough to love so fiercely that your
intensity can't withstand the force of your desires for
each other
and before too long
you end up killing each other before the year is even
out

an attempt was made

you and i were never meant to make it
we met with the same wandering lonely hearts
and with the same stubborn amount of hope

i was far too optimistic
you were far too pragmatic

we tried to make it work
because that is what hopeful love is supposed to do

we tried so very hard
until our kisses shortened
and two hopeful spoons would come to sleep back to back
so very hopelessly

these walls do not house a home

is it too much to ask to be free to walk away from it all?
to check out of this place in time
and wake up as someone else?

you loved that i was always here for you
and even now
even so far away from me
you check in to see if i am still here
and you know that i am
which is why you sleep so soundly
and exactly why i hate to look in the mirror

you know that i can't stand living with your ghost
and it haunts every room in this goddamn house that
we used to call our home

is it too much to ask to be free from this life that we
were building together?
to forget that we ever tried at all
to be able to remember only the hopeful potential of
love still yet to be found?

is it too much to ask to hit delete on it all?
to start again with someone new
to avoid the emotions that have moved in with your
ghost

is it too much to ask to finally disappear?

let it burn

depending on the day of the week love can set any sort of fire it so pleases

we tend to forget that desire and hope can both burn out equally

hope protects you

if i could
somehow
take away the hope that you have for him now
you might understand why i sound so defeated
whenever you call me to check-in

something real just happened between us
and he is a filter to the darkness that i now must live in

you better pray that he doesn't disappear as you did

the hunting darkness

when that darkness inside of you rose to the surface
i was there to help pull you out
every single time

a smile
a kiss
a joke
some words about our future together
whatever it would take to beat that motherfucker back
down

and now that you are gone
wouldn't you know it
but that darkness has decided to hunt me down in your
place
and i have no more hopeful stories to tell

the weight

in this new reality, a ring and a memory can weigh down a soul
just as much as gravity itself

my heart has turned

a million inspiring quotes about love cannot resurrect a heart that has chosen to kill itself

pandora

call it a reflex
a survival instinct
or a silly thing to do
but i don't dare look at a photo of you and i anymore

eventually

place the memory of me in a box made of tempered glass

move this history of ours to a corner of your mind
a place that you promised me you would never forget about

but i know that you will

remember what mother said

no one wants to hear about your bleeding heart

they want to hear of your strength
your focus
your drive
your will
your optimism
your hope

no one wants to hear your raw truth

and yet they still ask you what is wrong when you choose to say nothing at all

feet off the floor

i lay in bed
staring at the ceiling
putting off yet another day

i wonder if you are doing the same

probably not

why would you?
you got what you wanted
you got away from us
right?

i don't mean to assume
perhaps you are staring at the ceiling
just like me
maybe this isn't what you wanted after all

is this hopeful thinking
or is it wishful?

hard to tell anymore

but if you are melancholic
and angry
and defeated *right now*
then maybe we can share something
just one more time

fool me once

i am trying to hold you closer than this
and i can tell that you are struggling to hold me tighter
as well
but all these fucking knives in our hearts are preventing
us from bridging the distance between us two lovers

undone

you have been gone for over a week now and it has
been close to two months since you placed me on this
unexpected journey of mine

i knew that text was coming
it had to be

of course, you would look back on us when he left you
in the dark

i said that i was like an old pair of shoes that you were
too afraid to get rid of
you said that i was wrong
you said that i was more like your favorite sweater

and here i am
falling apart at the seams
while you pull on the stitching
even from so far away
still too afraid to let me go

sour

how did we ever forget that love comes with an expiration date?

this is how it goes

i think that it's time that we try to forget about all our sunny days together
it's time that we disconnect from all the laughing and the lovemaking
and the comfort found in two souls promising to be there for each other forever

it's time that we attempt to bury all these smiles
it's time to deny the longing glances shot from across the room to our bedroom

it's way past time that we remove ourselves from this home that we had built up together
and all those beautiful creature comforts that we always took for granted

it's time that one became two again
and time to forget that we ever knew each other at all

it's time for me to become the very thing you said i would never be
it's time for me to take my place among your fading memories

we could try

can we just pretend that our love will be enough to last the rest of our lives?

i can't stay here

i know that it's time to put on my walking shoes once again
the clock has been burning for weeks now
and i have been hanging out in the past
like a drunkard in a rundown bar
just hoping for a change

i know that it's time to brace myself for the great unknown once again
the wolves have been clawing at the door for weeks now
and i have been hiding under these covers like a child
deathly afraid of the monster under the bed
hoping it will all go away

i know that it's time to close the book on us
once again
i have been re-reading the same pages for weeks now
like a man lost in distraction and daydreams
just trying to get through one more day
hoping that your ghost might finally leave me alone

i know that it's time to move on
once again
but i really don't want to

you will be missed

you always asked me how much i loved you

enough that i am still here
and still hoping that i might
somehow
survive this heartache

just one more conversation

let's talk about the things that we are going to miss
about each other
that should take a lifetime
then you won't ever have to leave

lying in wait

i always told you they were wolves
you always told me not to worry
they were harmless
they were *just friends*

look how they tore your heart apart after i left

i wish that you could have been right this time around

gemma

the raspberry plant that we put in the backyard together
the one we called *'gemma'*
is doing very well

remember when you plucked some berries from it
and you said
'let's make some raspberry gemma'

god
that was so fucking cute of you

just one more silly reason to miss you
and that's just how life is for me now that you are gone

time and space

i have surrendered to all of you ghosts

i let my heart speak to yours
i watched as your belief in us broke down and crumbled under the weight of it all

then
my precious loves

i watched helplessly
as you all went off to build happy lives with someone else

and it was on those days that i finally felt the real distance between us
and yet
the filament forever remains between us

love is like

if love is like a knife then it is one that cuts both dull and deeply
leaving scar tissue where most other cuts would heal completely

if love is like a knife then it is one coated in a poison called *memories*
leaving a heartache so complete that it overshadows the sun itself

if love is like a knife then it is one aimed directly at my heart
and you are the one choosing to run it right through me

just make sure to leave some room for the others

it happens over time

at first, the distance forming is far too small to notice
unless you manage to catch the momentary flicker of
sadness in her eyes

after a while, the distance grows large enough for both
of you to see
and you both stay silent with no one wanting to talk
about it

then one day she is on a plane
and you are still right here
wishing that you didn't have to say goodbye for the last
time

wish you were here

i miss you when you are home

i miss you when you are gone

i miss you even when i don't think that i miss you at all

and then something as stupid as a plane in the sky kills me
like a comet to my heart

and it is right then that i remember taking you to the airport one final time

out there

hope is a heart i have yet to find

never forget

every single one who had my heart desired to be the
only one that ever had it

but you all were given a piece of me to forever keep
and that will always be just how deeply i loved you all

i can only hope that you loved with the same foolish
optimism that i did

write this down

sometimes you will feel as if you cannot weather
another storm
raining down your happiest memories with her

other times you will find yourself numb from the cold
air that her absence brings in its wake

but there will be days
like this one
where you will find yourself inspired by the anger
at just how fast she moved on
and on those days
a pen will be needed

keep this in mind

tread carefully upon my heart my love
for i have been known to write down notes in a book
and you might not want to be remembered for what
you *really* are

it's there

can you feel it?
the subtle change in the air

as if the love we shared has slightly cracked or frayed at the edges

not enough to see but it hurts just enough to feel
and even though you are still here planning our wedding
i am quietly asking myself
how much longer can we possibly have left?

water in my lungs

i know that you are worried about me

old habits die hard

i still worry about you too

but it's not enough to do what needs to be done to save this drowning love of ours

not ready to care

hope requires us to say that our best life is still ahead of us

it demands that we have some faith in the order to be found in the chaos

it asks us to believe in love
just one more time

but right now
i'm still not sure if i am going to listen to anything hope has to say at all

don't you see?

the problem isn't you
or me

it's us

your side

they rally against you now that you are no longer here with me

they tell me why i am better off without you

they pull hopeful quotes from the air like cheap parlor trick magicians

they try so very hard to get me to see the great life that i have ahead of me now that you are no longer here

they are keeping themselves quite busy trying to speak louder than my sadness

and all i want is someone to silently cry with
because i haven't even allowed myself to cry about all this just yet
and all because my heart still rallies to your side

it still holds onto some hope that this really isn't happening

our contract

i want out of our agreement

the one that states that my heart will still long for you
long after you are gone

long after you have moved on

this terribly unfair agreement of ours
where you get to tell me how well you are doing
and i must find the strength to lie to you in return

i know it's not good

i almost broke down right now thinking of you

i know that it will happen a few more times today
and tomorrow
and most likely the next day as well

who knows when this cycle will finally end?

maybe it won't

and that is the fear that i carry with me now

the fear

i hope that i don't live up to your final words

where are you?

i know
deep down
that i am not unlovable

i know
that somewhere out there is another lonely and
beautiful soul walking around broken
having conversations with ghosts

ghost therapy

don't overthink any of this
it can't be quite as sad as it seems
can it?
don't you dare overanalyze this
but you know that you always do

what could i have done differently this time around?
why do i keep losing the ones that i love?
why do i keep ending up in this lonely place?
why am i still here wondering why at all?

i know that i am overthinking this
because that is what i always do
having conversations with all of you
as if this were an *AA* meeting for my apparent
addiction to disappointing the ones that i offer my heart
to

you are no longer there to hear any of my words to you
but i secretly speak them to you all anyway

you stopped looking in my direction a long time ago
but i still check over my shoulder
like a bad habit
to see if i might catch you glancing back at me

you turned off the lights on us
but here i stay
forever fumbling in the dark
just trying to turn those lights back on
so that i might eventually find my way back home

stop overthinking this
you know what you need to do
but i also know that i am addicted to these meetings
that i have with you all

afterword
by ryan donnelly

---

*I*n my youth, I regarded love and loss as a great final thing. Every ending was the last true love that I would ever allow myself to experience, but as time would continually remind me, I was not in control of the desires of my heart, and my heart would forever hold onto a stubborn hope that it would eventually find another spark to match its own.

And so I would continue to search for love in the absence of the word because my heart always held close an ember of hope that could never fully extinguish, no matter the intensity of the cold storms that my spirit would have to endure in the absence of her affection.

As time moved ahead as time always does it became clear to me that there were lessons to learn here. I knew that if I was going to recapture temperamental happiness and trusting love before my last breath was drawn that I would have to start acknowledging the gifts and lessons to be found in the echoes of lost love.

There is just no way to minimize the hurt felt by the funeral of a friend, and that is what the death of love will always be to me; not just a death of who we once were, but of who we could have been, it is the ending of a dream, and for many, this is all they can see, *the end*. There was a time when that was all I could see as well.

I grew to listen more than react.
I found a stillness that allowed for true self-reflection.
I opened up to faith in something more than that which I thought I could control.
I learned to let love go because I finally understood that one cannot own love at all. That love is an ethereal thing, both limitless and impossible to capture in a frame of time.
I saw all of these moments as just moments to be grateful for because they were my moments to remember; *the good, the bad, and the impossible.*

I see now that the loss of love is not a great final thing at all. It is not the ending of the story, it is simply the end of a chapter in the living book that is our life.

Such a loss is a rebirth, one that we cannot see or appreciate until we are ready to accept the temporary nature of everything. It is the ending of who you once knew to make way for who you have always been destined to be. It is sad, *I know*, but it is hopeful as well. It just takes time to see that.

Seasons change as they always will, and we must surrender to the will of a hand that we do not control.

We have time and that little ember that rests in all of us. We have hope, and that will always be enough… *it has to be.*

conversations with ghosts

conversations with ghosts

hope

Manufactured by Amazon.ca
Bolton, ON